AF573813

To all the children in the Royal Berkshire Hospital

Royalties from sales of this book will be donated to the Royal Berkshire Hospital

Also by John Talbot and published by Simon & Schuster Young Books:

The Great Tabascoes
Hardback ISBN 0-7500-0299-9 Paperback ISBN 0-7500-0303-0
Pins and Needles
Hardback ISBN 0-7500-0376-6 Paperback ISBN 0-7500-0377-4
Bunny Pulls It Off
Hardback ISBN 0-7500-0763-X Paperback ISBN 0-7500-0764-8

First published in Great Britain in 1992 by
Simon & Schuster Young Books
Campus 400
Maylands Avenue
Hemel Hempstead
Herts HP2 7EZ

Typeset in 18pt Century Schoolbook by Goodfellow & Egan Ltd, Cambridge
Printed and bound in Belgium by Proost International Book Productions

A catalogue record for this book is available from the British Library

ISBN 0-7500-0765-6
ISBN 0-7500-0766-4 (pb)

DOCTOR DOG

written and illustrated by

John Talbot

SIMON & SCHUSTER
YOUNG BOOKS

Doctor Dog was in a bit of a flap. He had been up all night visiting a sick hamster, and this morning he had a lot of patients waiting to see him.
It was going to be another busy day for Doctor Dog.

His first patient was little Emmanuel Mouse. "He's been wheezing all night," said Mrs Mouse anxiously.

"Pull up your shirt," said Doctor Dog impatiently, "and let me listen to your chest."

Just then the 'phone started to ring.
Ring ring! Ring ring!
"Oh, that does sound bad," said Doctor Dog.
"I'll prescribe something strong for you,
my lad... Next patient!"

A moment later in bustled Hilda Hen.
"Well, doctor," began Hilda, rather embarrassed, "I'm having trouble with my feathers. They're coming out."

"You're moulting," said Doctor Dog gruffly. "It's quite normal for a hen of your age. I'll prescribe some ointment for you to rub well in... Next patient!"

xpecting another baby.
Dog.
thing too tiring."

ight home and rest!"

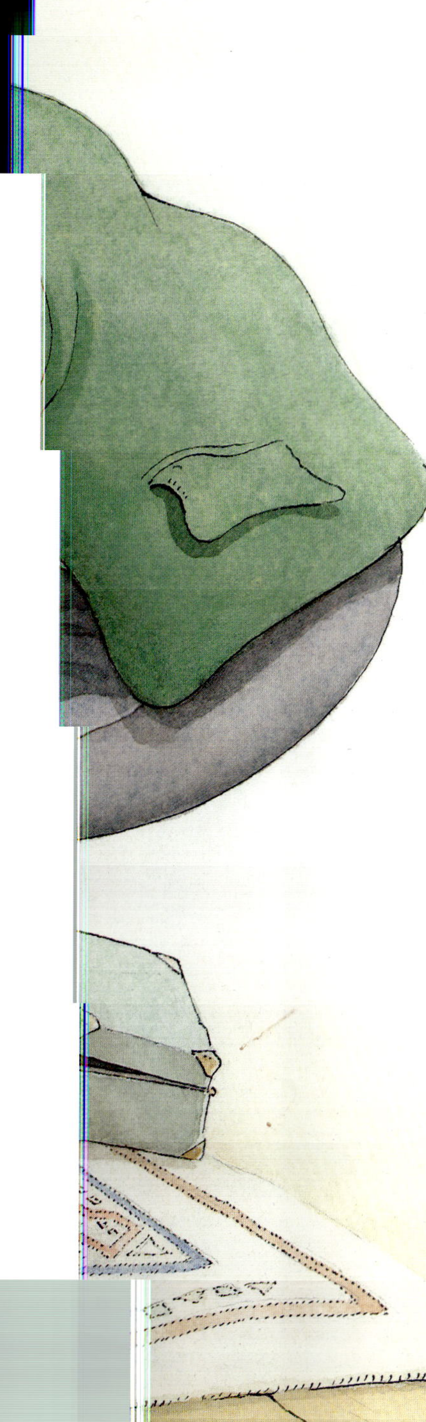

Later on, while Old Riley the Chemist was preparing their medicine, the ladies were talking.
"Doctor Dog was a little snappy this morning," said Mrs Mouse.

Doctor Dog

anice. "I'll think of

Later that same evening,
Janice made some secret
'phone calls.

When Doctor Dog arrived at the surgery next morning, he was surprised to find nobody there.

Doctor Dog had lost his patience. "This is the last straw!" he yelled. A moment later, the 'phone rang. "Yes!" snapped Doctor Dog.

It was a miserable afternoon for Doctor Dog. Nobody came to the surgery, nobody was at home in the village, and by the time he arrived at Dame Veronica's mansion, he was fed up and more than a little sorry for himself.

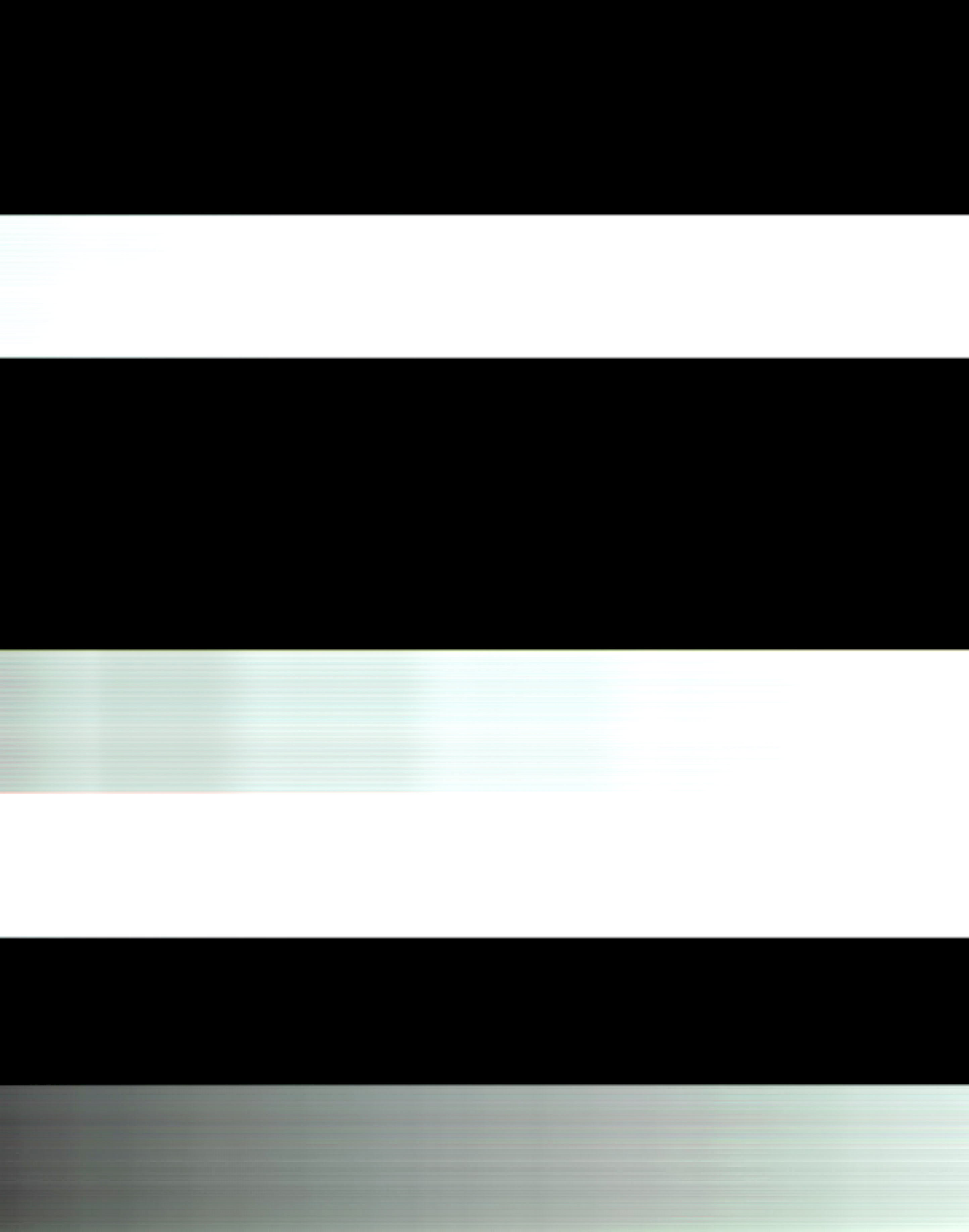

He walked slowly up the stairs to Dame Veronica's room.
Suddenly the door burst open ...

"Surprise! Surprise! Hooray!"
Doctor Dog was astonished.
He could see all his patients.
And there was Janice!

“We decided to throw you a party, Doctor Dog,” said the lag-goose, “to thank you for looking after us all.”

“Well,” cried Doctor Dog, “this is just the medicine I need! Pass the sausage rolls!”

Doctor Dog had a wonderful time.
But towards the end of the party Janice tapped him on the shoulder and whispered,
"Quick, Doctor! Tabitha is having kittens!"
Doctor Dog grabbed his bag and followed Janice.
Soon he had delivered not one, not *two*...but *THREE* beautiful new kittens: Otis, Mitzi and Muffin.
"It's been a day full of surprises," laughed Doctor Dog,
"but this one is the best of all!"